MW00891392

FLEET WEEK IN NYC

Written by
ROBIN F. JOHNSON
Illustrated by
Danijela Popovic

For United States Navy Captain Owen G. Thorp III
(1954-2017)
Thank you for your service.

And to Suzan DeLambily Hale,
who inspired this picture book.

©2018 by Robin F. Johnson
All Rights Reserved

ISBN-13:978-1721712694
ISBN-10:1721712690

Cover art and illustrations by Danijela Popovic
All characters and events in this book are fictitious. Any
resemblance to persons living or dead is strictly coincidental.

 Bearly
Tolerable
Publications

The following provided information for insuring accuracy in the
information and illustrations. Any inaccuracies are due to the
publisher and not to the experts below.

Thank You!
CAPT Eric McCartney, U.S. Navy
Arlyn Danielson,Chief Curator, USCG
Sgt. Dallas T. Jackson USMC

Every year at the end of May, New York City hosts a patriotic party for more than 2,000 United States Navy sailors, Coast Guard members, and Marines who have recently returned from serving overseas.

This celebration is known as Fleet Week.

Fleet Week, which has been a tradition in New York City since 1984, provides the brave men and women of the Navy, Coast Guard, and Marines with an opportunity to share their day-to-day adventures with New Yorkers.

And it also gives New Yorkers a chance to thank those who protect and maintain our ports, harbors, and world waterways.

This weeklong maritime festival kicks off with the
spectacular Parade of Ships. Active military ships,
cutters, patrol boats, and command vessels
maneuver along the Hudson River from
Battery Park to just south of the
George Washington Bridge.

The visiting ships change every year, but the
highlight is always when the flagship, carrying the
commanders from the three branches of sea services,
cruises by Fort Hamilton and is greeted with a gun salute.

Fun and Free
is a theme for Fleet Week.
The public is invited, at no charge, to tour recently deployed ships
at various locations around the boroughs.

And as the public goes "aboard" the ships, the sea-faring men and women of the Navy, Coast Guard, and Marines step "ashore." They are eager to meet you and to pose for photos.

A highlight of Fleet Week takes place in Times Square, where an enormous clear dive tank is constructed so that Navy divers can demonstrate their SCUBA skills.

Look closely at the tank and you'll discover that tic-tac-toe boards have been painted on the sides.
Children and adults have fun challenging the divers to play.

And while Fleet Week events and venues sometimes change, usually in Times Square you'll see a martial arts demonstration by the Marines, a silent drill team performance by the Coast Guard, and a band concert by the Navy.

Liberty Park in Jersey City, NJ, becomes a military base during Fleet Week. The Coast Guard conducts a search and rescue mission; Navy divers demonstrate how to defuse underwater explosives, and Marines give the public tours of military vehicles and personnel equipment.

Coast Guard members also jump from helicopters into the water and entertain spectators with fast rope climbing demonstrations.

Physical fitness is an important part of military excellence. The servicemen and servicewomen of the Navy, Coast Guard, and Marines are in tip-top shape.

During Fleet Week, the Navy usually challenges the New York Police Department to a friendly game of rugby, and all three branches of the sea services take part in the Freedom Run, a 1.7 mile fun run through the Financial District and ending at 9/11 Memorial Plaza. On Marine Day, children and adults alike are invited to test their own fitness by working out with the Marines.

During Fleet Week, you will see these servicemen and servicewomen eating at restaurants, walking along the streets, jogging in the parks, and visiting museums and theaters.

Yet they still take the time to read to children at local libraries,
and for the past several years, they have
helped to build houses for
Habitat for Humanity.

Many other port cities across the country host celebrations like the Big Apple's Fleet Week: San Francisco, Fort Lauderdale, San Diego, Seattle, Los Angeles, Baltimore, and Portland, to name a few.

Each celebration is a little different. In San Francisco, for example, the Navy and Marine's flight demonstration squadron, the Blue Angels, dazzles spectators with its aerial acrobatics.

In Fort Lauderdale, the Coast Guard Station hosts a memorial service for the survivors of Pearl Harbor. In Seattle the Navy organizes a camp out and kids' carnival, and in Portland children and adults compete in the popular milk carton boat race, where human-powered boats that float only by means of milk cartons and jugs compete in nine different categories.

In the end, New Yorkers can't help but be reminded that their Fleet Week gala is celebrated the week before Memorial Day, a national holiday where our citizens remember, with appreciation, those who died in the armed forces.

To the Navy, Coast Guard, and Marines, New York City welcomes you to Fleet Week and thanks you for your service.

GLOSSARY and IMPORTANT WORDS

MARITIME -- having to do with ocean navigation or trade

UNITED STATES NAVY -- a branch of the United States Armed Forces. The Navy maintains, trains, and equips sailors to ensure the freedom of the seas.

UNITED STATES COAST GUARD -- a branch of the United States Armed Forces. Members are responsible for maritime safety and security, search and rescue, ice operations, environmental protection, and defense readiness.

UNITED STATES MARINE CORPS -- a branch of the United States Armed Forces. Marines are responsible for conducting amphibious (land and sea) operations together with the U.S. Navy.

CUTTER -- single-masted sailing vessel

FLAGSHIP -- a ship carrying the flag officer or commander of a fleet or squadron

FORT HAMILTON -- located in Brooklyn and built in 1831. Currently a military installation for the Army National Guard and the United States Army Reserve.

DEPLOYED -- prepared for readiness

SCUBA -- a portable breathing device that consists of a mouthpiece, hose, and one or two tanks of compressed air strapped on the back. Self-Contained Underwater Breathing Apparatus.

LIBERTY PARK -- a recreational park located in Jersey City, NJ, with ferry service to Ellis Island and to the Statue of Liberty. Liberty Park maintains a science center, outdoor performance area, a picnic area, and a two-mile promenade.

ABOUT THE AUTHOR

Robin Johnson is a former educator; during her twenty-year career, she worked with students from every grade level – kindergarten through college. She received numerous grants to enhance school libraries. Robin holds a BA from Colgate University in English and Education, an MA from Stanford University in English Literature, and advanced certification from Columbia University's Institute on the Teaching of Writing. In her spare time, she enjoys power-walking, needlepoint, Scrabble, and anything that glitters! Robin lives with her husband in Beach Haven, NJ, and in New York City, NY.
She is also the author of
"First Grade's Forever,"
which is available on
AMAZON.

ABOUT THE ILLUSTRATOR

Drawing is something that Danijela Popovic has loved since she could hold a pencil. After finishing high school for industrial design, she graduated with a degree in illustration from the Academy of Arts in Banja Luka (Bosnia and Herzegovina). She started to draw digitally in 2011, and since then she's worked as a freelance illustrator and digital artist. For the last four years, she's been illustrating books for children, and that makes her happy.

13467633R00017

Made in the USA
Lexington, KY
31 October 2018